THE POCKET BOOK OF QUOTES

An Actor's Guide To Motivation

Ronald 'Wink' Woodall

Published and distributed in the United States by The Talent Connect, Garden City, New York

Cover Design – Bookney Inc.
Editing and Layout – Pen Publish Profit, LLC
Interior Design – www.queekpub.com
ISBN 13: 979-8-9860886-0-0
LCCN: 2022906489

Printed in the United States of America
www.thetalentconnect.com

I DEDICATE THIS BOOK TO...

This book is dedicated to you, the true 'Creative' taking the initiative to grow as you embark on this forever-changing journey to find your niche in the field of life. You may not always be sure about your surroundings, but you can always put in the work to be confident about yourself.

As a Talent pursuing the big dream and taking the leap to become an actor, there are many implications and verbal messages that, at times, may leave you discouraged. This can reflect in your overall performance and ultimately interfere with your process.

This book of quotes is here to help challenge those internal thoughts while offering a perspective and fuel for positive self-talk that allows one to put their best foot forward.

FOREWORD

I've learned through many trials and tribulations that we can manifest greatness by lifting each other. I found my way to success by reading about the wins of our ancestors. Knowing that they made a way out of no way inspired me. Their stories gave me a blueprint for living, learning, and giving. I owe so much to people I've never met. What I believe they would want us all to do is to pay their gifts forward for future generations. That is the power of motivation. It's eternal. It's a gift that keeps on giving. When you motivate someone, you ignite a positive future. Our world deserves a positive future. The good news is that we already possess everything required to be great. It starts with motivation.

The world is full of things that can motivate us to become the best version of ourselves. These special moments in life come when we slow down and take the time to be fully present. That is where the greatness is, right in between the doubt, the fears, the anger, and the desperation. Greatness is a part of who we are. Each day is a gift and what we do with that gift is how we give back. The Pocket Book of Quotes: An Actor's Guide to Motivation is one such gift. The words on the following pages are designed to lift you and those you love. God blesses us all to turn our dreams and ideas into their tangible equivalents. To manifest the best of who we are, we must have faith, be willing to do the work, and expect the outcomes. As you read the contents of this book, be sure to share what you learn with others. Your life will change right before you as you take in the words and apply them to your life.

Remember, we all can be and do great things. If you find that you cannot do great things, make up your mind to do small things in a great way. This is the path of uplift that will empower future generations. It is no longer enough that we survive; it is time to develop and prosper.

This work is ours to do. It begins with you and what you tell yourself and those you love each day you rise. We are the dreams of our ancestors. Finally, remember that we win not because we are great. We win because God is great. Now read on, be lifted, and pay the blessings forward as you motivate future generations.

BK Fulton, Founding Chairman
& CEO, Soulidifly Productions

A WORD FROM THE AUTHOR

Who doesn't like encouragement when you embark on a journey to put yourself out there and receive critique on what you can do as an actor or actress?

In my career, I have worked with many actors, actresses, directors, students, and others in the entertainment and education industries. Many have said the same things:

1. I'm nervous.
2. I don't think I can do it.
3. Send me some positive energy before this meeting.
4. Any words of encouragement?

Hearing this and much more, my thoughts were: "how about creating something pocket-sized that can be used for wisdom and encouragement for those looking to put their best foot forward as they pursue their next big break?" From there, the idea of The Pocket Book of Quotes was born.

The quotes are inspired by The Talent Connect (TTC) guiding principles applicable to those who may need a reminder of how to remain grounded and how to navigate through the terrain during their pursuit to accomplish their goals in this industry. This book will provide you with:

1. A voice that will help preserve a positive mindset throughout the ups and downs of the acting business.

2. The confidence to walk into any room to perform at an optimal level

3. Quotes generated for actors but are helpful to anyone in any industry.

TTC and I recognize that the acting community needs emotional support and strength to be prepared for the demands of this business. Far too often, actors don't receive the necessary feedback to help them understand their strengths and weaknesses, therefore, they may proceed aimlessly or internalize unfortunate circumstances (i.e., auditions that didn't go their way) causing Talent to second guess themselves and hesitate when it comes to putting their best foot forward. These quotes aim to redirect faulty thinking toward a more realistic perspective. The ultimate goal is to help shift any potential idea that you are always the reason an audition "didn't work out in your favor." We want to help reinforce or help you re-imagine yourself as one of several conditional business factors that must be considered when it comes to booking a role.

If you are being called in for an audition, you've already caught their attention. Great Job! Your next task is to have the best mindset possible so you can put on the best performance possible.

The remainder of the process is up to the rest of the factors involved.

Keep this book near, read it often and share it with your fellow friends in the industry.

Enjoy!

Wink

x

Let's keep it, Reel.
For the most part, there
are no rules...
Just mainly etiquette...

The "rules" change all the time. It's human nature to observe someone else's experience and assume that if you apply the same formula, you should receive the same results. We are often seeking standards that tend to change daily. Subjectivity is thrown into every single component of decision-making, it makes it almost impossible to believe that the same pathway will garner the same success all the time. So many want to know:

What do casting directors want to see?

Should I greet the CD?

Can I send a follow-up email?

Do I mention that we've crossed paths on social media as a conversation starter, etc....?

You'll often learn that the rules differ depending on who you are dealing with. You may hear a common preference on how to handle yourself, but you'll often find that it varies. Pay attention to etiquette but you can also use discretion to bend the "rules" from time to time...

CONTENTS

A DIFFERENT
PERSPECTIVE

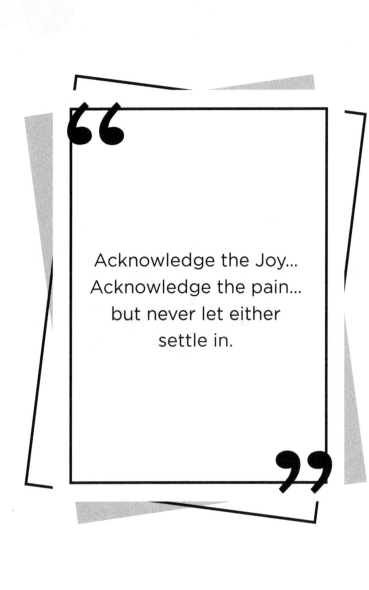

Acknowledge the Joy...
Acknowledge the pain...
but never let either
settle in.

This business is full of ups and downs... Be aware of both if they shall reveal themselves. Either way, never let them define you. Find a way to note each circumstance and then put them aside. For example, you may book a role on your favorite show. That's amazing! Enjoy that great feeling; talk about it; receive that moment. But don't lose the hunger and don't change how you got there. Move on and get right back to work. On the flip side, if you didn't get that role, you were confident your audition alone would lead you to, acknowledge the disappointment but continue back on the grind. If there were notes given by the Casting Director, then look to apply them the next time around. If not, keep it moving. Whether it be joyful or painful, put that feeling aside so you can continue to progress through your journey.

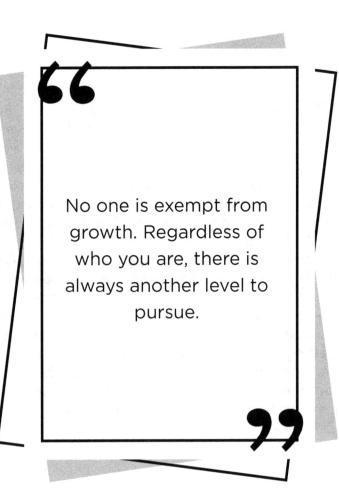

No one is exempt from growth. Regardless of who you are, there is always another level to pursue.

We are all human before the titles that often supersede us. Just like you, a casting director, producer, manager, agent, and or any professional you deem of prominent stature, all have another level to strive for. Jay Z, one of the best rappers to have ever done it, is hailed to be one at the top of the rap pinnacle; but he wasn't done with his life endeavors. He ventured into several other realms of interest to conquer, like entrepreneurship. That is a new pocket that he has sought to conquer as well. If he gets to a level where he feels he's met his goal, you better believe he will enter another realm if he has not already. It doesn't matter what level we're on, we are all human and are seeking greatness above us. Walking into the casting office, we should always keep that in mind. The people behind the camera making the decisions are also human and we share a common goal to get better in life. This should help ease the pressure of your pursuit in the room because we all have places we are trying to reach, and this is a place where everyone in that room can relate.

There is a difference
between confidence and
cockiness.

Understand the thin line between the two states of being: confidence and cockiness. When you are confident, you are sure of yourself, your abilities, and the things you may need to improve. Confidence exudes positively and is usually well-received by most. Confident beings are less likely to care about outside opinions. On the other hand, cockiness appears as overconfident. This person may not realize it, but they are often not self-secure and must lead with a chip on their shoulder to prove something to others. A cocky personality makes sure that everyone is aware and craves dominance over others. Their focus is less on personal growth and more on finding one's dominant space in a community. There is an external dependence which is often the reason they are boastful and brag often. It is imperative to be aware of your personality and what drives it. Cockiness is a turn-off in the casting room while confidence is infectious and magnetic.

Learn not to run from
fear but to embrace it.

Fear can be one of your greatest allies if you accept it for what it is. Fear has many benefits: alertness, adrenalin rush, opportunity, etc. Fear is a natural human response. Actors are encouraged to accept that it is a part of their process of stepping into a new zone, not running away from it but moving alongside it.

Step outside of the box,
there is so much more
room out here.

So many life messages teach us to stay within parameters. Just because these messages exist, doesn't mean you have to live by them. The box is often a perceived set of rules that don't exist but hold value because most people live inside of it. But that doesn't have to be the case. In fact, for many who are brave enough to venture outside of the box, more stories are being told of newfound freedom with limitless possibilities. So many people live inside the box which makes it challenging to move around while inside. There is so much more room outside of the box.

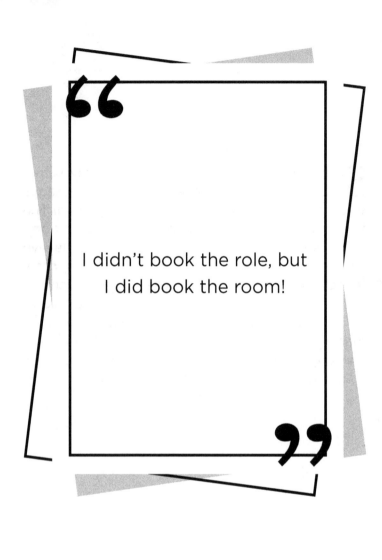

I didn't book the role, but
I did book the room!

Perspective is key. How often have you "killed" (did well) an audition but didn't book the actual role? This happens to most successful talent. You may not have booked that role but now you have a set of fans within that casting office that want to find a place for your talent. It's important that you see the bigger picture. It's all about perspective...

Sometimes an opportunity is an opportunity for the right opportunity.

It is very possible that you may audition for one role and walk out of the room with a shot for a different role that may even be a better fit. Casting Directors and Producers are often looking for something specific. While you may do an amazing job on the audition, you may also be considered for a different character that may fit you better. Be open to notes and directions given by those in the room. You may really like the role you walked in for, but you may fall in love with another role they really see you for. Keep an open mind for the right opportunity.

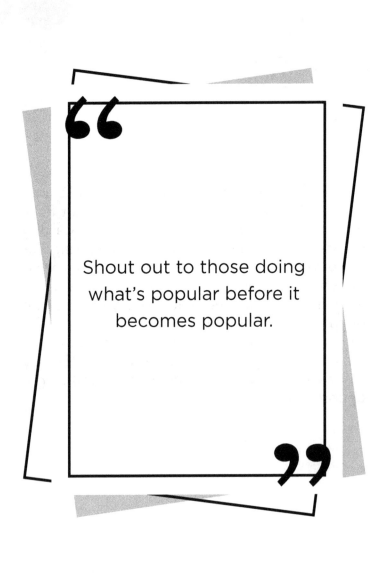

Shout out to those doing what's popular before it becomes popular.

Be a trendsetter and not a wave rider. Be a trendsetter rather than a trend servant by doing what is popular before it becomes popular. You don't always have to follow everyone else because it's popular. Doing something unique, different, and new can be lonely and nerve-wracking but it can also be the pathway to a fresh and new way for others to gravitate toward and follow your lead. How dope would that be?

ACTING/AUDITION TIPS

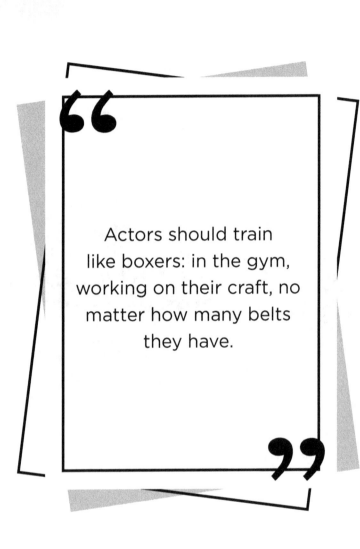

Actors should train
like boxers: in the gym,
working on their craft, no
matter how many belts
they have.

When have you ever heard of a boxer who won all their fights without training? Floyd Mayweather, arguably one of the greatest boxers to have ever done it, has always trained harder for each fight like he had something to lose. The late great Kobe Bryant is infamous for his "Mamba Mentality" approach to each game. Regardless of how successful he was or how high the regard other players held him, he would still push himself to train before and after each game. Competition is real in the acting world. There are so many conditions involved in what makes an actor great. It is your responsibility to continue to enrich your craft. You are great but there will always be someone who can overtake your greatness. You protect this by always staying on top of your game: train, read, study... Do whatever it takes to keep yourself on a growth plan. It can only continue to help you.

Just go in, do the work,
and get out.

As an actor, your role is to get in that room, kill that audition, get out, and get ready for the next... No need for the extra... No worrying, contemplating, or second guessing. Be prepared: do the research, understand your character, the relationships, and the direction of the scene, be on time, do the audition, take notes or directions, and then get out. Do not sit around the casting room making small talk. That's the best way to ruin an experience. The most excellent way to make the case for yourself is simply doing the work.

Everyone's process is different.

It's important to understand that we are all unique in our own way. Whatever it took actor one to get a role on their favorite show will likely take actor two a different set of steps to get to the same place. Like the palm of a hand, many of us may appear identical but we all have a "fingerprint" type of difference that may not always be overtly apparent. Certain qualities may be slightly different. It is important to lean into your strengths and show them what you are working with. Don't expect the same experience as someone else.

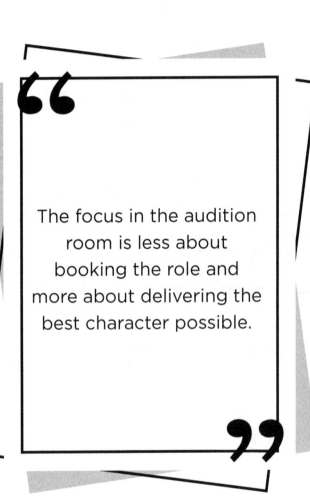

" The focus in the audition room is less about booking the role and more about delivering the best character possible. "

You can't directly control one's decision to make you the final choice for the role. There are just too many factors involved. However, you can control how powerful you deliver your character... That in turn may lead to a choice being made in your favor. With your sole focus set on the strength of character, you are in complete control of delivering a solid audition.

Talent speaks for itself.

Let your work do the talking… It's so much more impressive to allow the work to show what you are capable of instead of your mouth explaining what you are hoping to present. If your work is as great as you say, then present it in the best fashion possible. Make sure it's well represented on every platform you expect views. This includes social media, casting profile sites, websites, etc. Your work gives the industry everything they need to know about your talent so please do more than just talk about it. Be about it.

Set personal goals for the audition room.

So many people report walking into the audition room with one thing in mind, booking. The problem with that is the actor personally doesn't have any control over anyone else's decision to offer you the role. However, one can set personal goals aligned with delivering a stellar performance. Those goals can become your targets in your audition. Then you are in a full position to decide how successful you are based on meeting those goals in that room.

Curiosity killed the cat
but simultaneously
created a beast.

Unleash the beast! Don't be afraid to ask questions! You may find the key to unlock that barrier that has held you back.

ACTING BUSINESS

Always remember that acting is a craft, but it is also a business.

Fundamental notes for actors on all levels:

Be professional!
Be prepared!
Be on time!
Be present in the moment!
Understand your character!
Follow audition instructions! (All of them)
Dress the part!

Dear Talent, the most powerful rep on your team is yourself.

You are the MVP! Your Agent's, Attorney's, Manager's, or PR Rep.'s role is to help facilitate the process. Your talent is what brings it all together. Understand your needs, and how the business operates, and provide your reps with as much materials that will help them push for you.

You want your talent rep to be one of your biggest fans.

On the business side, actors are the products, casting directors/producers/networks are the buyers, and talent representatives are the sellers. The more the seller (representative) believes in the talent, the more confident and assertive the approach that the representatives take. You can almost guarantee that your representative will not hold any punches when pitching or submitting you for a role if they are one of your biggest fans. It helps when the representative you choose is a fan of yours.

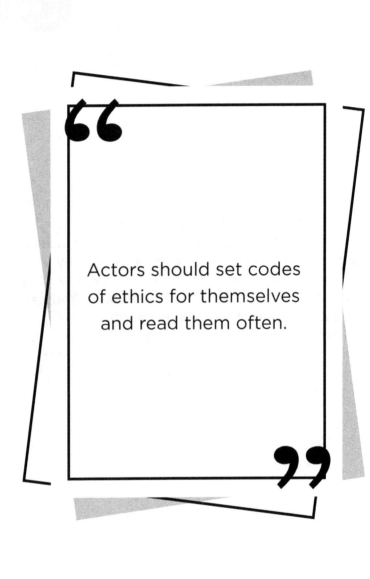

Actors should set codes
of ethics for themselves
and read them often.

To keep one connected to their moral compass and stay grounded after dealing with a lot of turmoil and stress, revisit the list of principles you set for yourself.

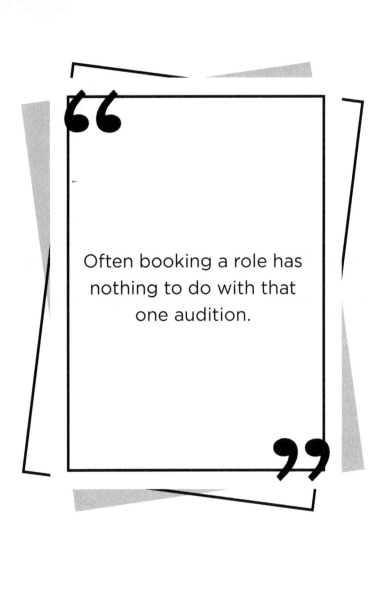

Often booking a role has nothing to do with that one audition.

It may take a series of encounters with casting directors before they learn your craft. Be consistent and apply the notes they give you.

Aim to become resourceful just as much as, if not more than, you manage to seek resources.

Actors with a well-rounded understanding of the other responsibilities attached to making a film have a better understanding of the entire process. With production experience, you may have an easier time understanding what the committee in the casting room is looking for from a technical standpoint. It can also give you insight into budgetary concerns and union rules as it applies to deal points and negotiation strategies. If you are a Talent new to acting, an understanding of the producer/writer/director roles can offer an independent production a valuable resource.

GROWTH MINDSET

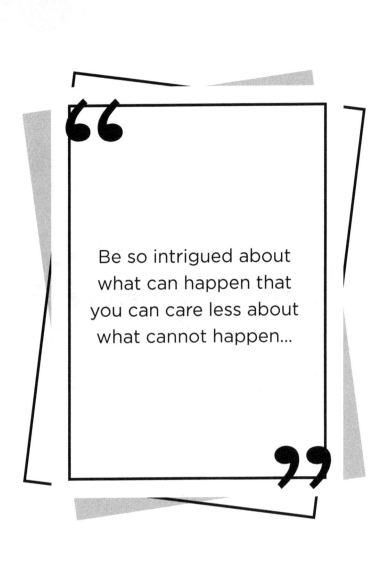

Be so intrigued about
what can happen that
you can care less about
what cannot happen...

Be intentional about committing your time to positive energy so much that you have less time to invest in negative energy. They both exist and either of them can take over your mindset. No human being is exempt from having negative thoughts. Living in that space often can completely zap one's energy and affect one's performance. It can take away constructive time that can be placed toward personal growth. The idea is to identify the strengths of a situation and build upon them. This kind of focus enhances the state of mind. It is also a form of encouragement that can lead toward more positive sources and outcomes. As positive thoughts accumulate in the forefront of your mindset, the negative thoughts take a backseat and ultimately become no match for the power of positivity. It's not that the negativity doesn't exist. They both exist. However, you have the power to choose which one you would like to lead your mindset. The goal is to invest more time in positivity, so negativity becomes a non-factor: allowing one to operate on their highest frequency."

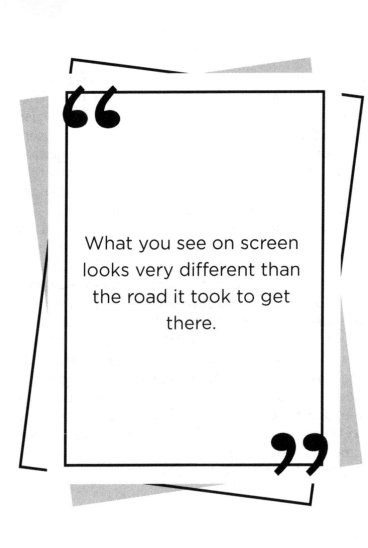

What you see on screen looks very different than the road it took to get there.

It's not all glitz and glam. Be committed to the whole process. Many want to get into the business because they see the fruits of the labor, but not many are prepared or are aware of the kind of road it may take to get there.

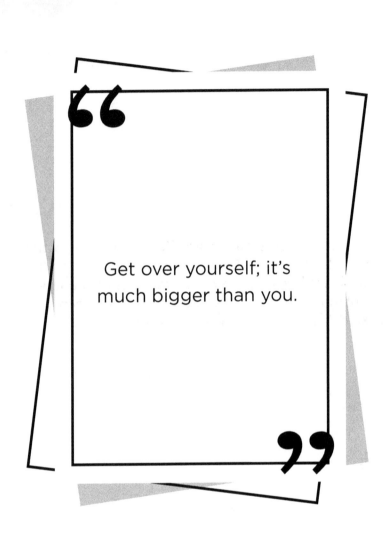

Get over yourself; it's much bigger than you.

It's not about you. It's about the overall process which also includes other factors: other actors, producers, crew, pre-production, post-production, distribution, etc.

Growth is abundant
outside of your comfort
zone.

When you are comfortable, you are not challenging yourself. It's easy to become bored in that space. There is no need to get excited if you don't push to get better. If you want to turn your talent up a notch, get outside of that comfort zone. It will help you learn new and exciting things about yourself that can help push you to the next level. If you are a great actor who feels very comfortable in your native language, why not study another language that will eventually enhance your overall profile?

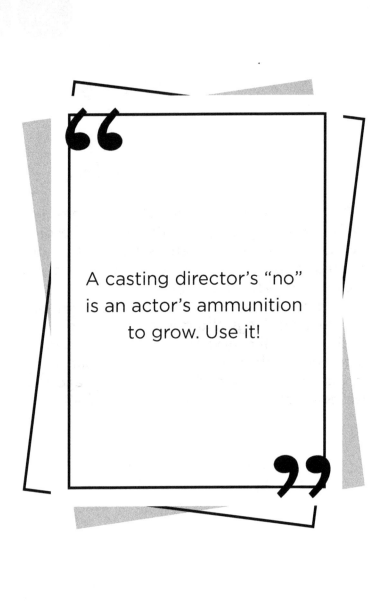

A casting director's "no"
is an actor's ammunition
to grow. Use it!

In the acting world, adversity can exist in so many places. We encourage actors to use it to propel forward. In the casting room, a "no" can have several meanings. Either way, it shouldn't hold one back from using it to get better. A 'no' with feedback offers one a reference to follow up on. Often, actors resurface in some of the same casting offices. This is an excellent opportunity to show the Casting Director how you applied the notes to their feedback.

Be inspired by the
possibilities.

If you can't be excited about what you have, get excited about what you will get! Be inspired!

Stay Motivated!

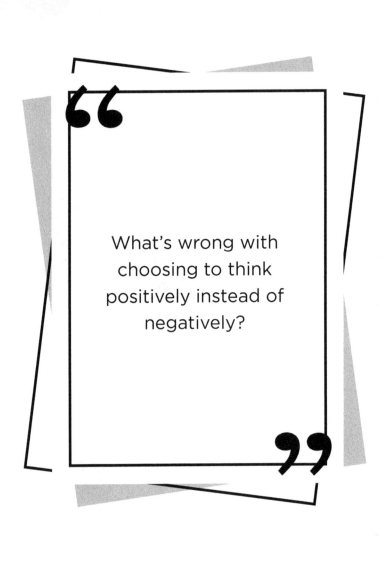

What's wrong with choosing to think positively instead of negatively?

What we decide to think about and how we think about it is our choice. So why not choose to think positively? If your argument is, "well I might be wrong if I try to think positively and then feel let down if I'm wrong. Then you may need to consider that you can also be wrong if you thought negatively about something and then the outcome ended up being positive. So, you spent much of your time passing negative energy through your body when you may not have to. Thinking negatively is a defense mechanism but it is highly stressful on the body. It can also deter desired outcomes before you even try. When you introduce a negative idea to your mind, you already start on the wrong foot which doesn't give you the greatest chance of conquering any challenge. But when you go in positively, even if it doesn't work out, at least you gave it your best shot possible.

Align your personal and professional brand.

In this day and age of acting, with the increased level of social media platforms and easy access to public figures, it is true that your audience may expect to know more about you outside of the acting world. It is not a requirement, but it has become a critical component that is often used by productions to help understand talent demographics, as well as help productions maximize viewership projections. There are several perspectives on this evolving factor, but the reality is that it does exist. If you have chosen to engage this component (social media) of your Talent profile, you are encouraged to include information about things you are passionate about, skills, hobbies, etc. Be mindful of what and how you reveal that personal information. Private information is what you don't have to disclose. Keep in mind that it may surface. You should always be prepared to explain it in a healthy way that does not hurt the integrity of your brand.

MOTIVATION
VALIDATION
PERSEVERANCE
(MVP)

If you believe in yourself
then they can too.

When someone walks into the room, it's not hard to tell how they feel about themselves. It starts from the greeting to the time you leave. You must lead with confidence: greetings, positive nature of the small conversation that precedes the audition, and of course the closing statement.

Get up, get back in that room, and do it again until you get it!

Keep pushing! Who told you it was going to be easy? Actors will inevitably hear "no" more frequently, than hearing "yes". Either response should not stop one's progress. Be resilient in your pursuit to present the best character. It will eventually happen if you continue to press forward and do it again.

Make sure you are always in progress.

With most journeys, there are peaks and valleys, ups and downs, ins and outs, and strengths and weaknesses. These momentum shifts can often present a misleading picture of your overall process. It's important to consider where your starting point was and how far you've come along. Realizing your progress alone can help reinforce the passion behind a tireless journey. The entertainment industry can offer some pretty heavy blows. Noting your progress and setting reasonable expectations can help foster an encouraging perspective that can recycle your passion to keep moving forward. You are not worrying about the setbacks as much as you are impressed with your progress. Set your own pace and keep pushing along. You'll get there when you are supposed to. Regardless of what level you are on, we can always improve something.

"

It's easy to watch from
the perimeter when no
one else is in the middle,
but it's hard to get in
the mix after everyone
has already jumped in.

"

Be fearless. Don't worry about who didn't try it first. Don't worry about what others think because you went first. Jump in and set the tone. Too often, you find actors waiting to see what everyone else is doing before they take their shot. Don't waste your time thinking about what others are doing, embrace the power of you and set the tone. Now everyone who goes after you must work around your statement. It's alright to jump in first. You may make such an impact that nothing else matters after you've made your mark.

Create self reflective
opportunities that
allow you to grow your
confidence.

The audition process can be grueling. Most actors are looking for some form of approval which usually comes from a callback or booking the role. Actors audition for roles and are at the mercy of the casting process. This can be nerve-wracking for talent waiting on a callback. While decisions must be made, it doesn't mean that actors can't create their own checks and balances systems to focus on. Redirecting one's anticipatory moment to reflect on personal audition goals makes for the perfect distraction from the common issue of waiting on a response for approval. Instead, actors can identify 1 to 3 indicators to set as improvement markers (i.e., did I project my voice at an appropriate level, did I take a beat after that monologue, did I have my eye lines right, did I have fun). No one needs permission to set their own goals which may at times be aligned with what the casting office is looking for. At the end of an audition, they can measure their success indicators to determine their success, ultimately fulfilling their intrinsic approval needs.

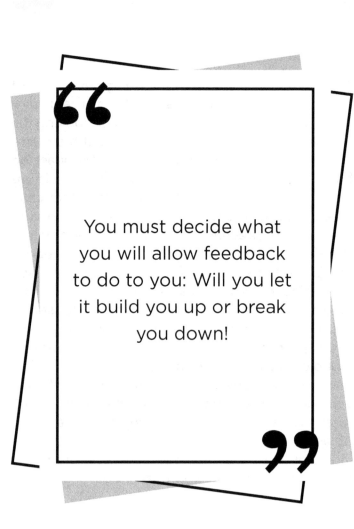

You must decide what you will allow feedback to do to you: Will you let it build you up or break you down!

Feedback can be one of your best tools or threats. It all depends on the perspective you take. Actors who have a growth mindset are always at their best when they allow feedback to build their level of preparedness for whatever comes next. They believe that the acting process is a journey, and an audition is a stop along the way: Each stop offers a new key that unlocks a new treasure for the next stop.

Be the vibe you seek.

Is it possible that the power you need already lies within you? Personal fulfillment is much more valuable than seeking approval from others. It is not necessary to search for others to be accepted. You already possess the potential to get it from yourself. Those who can organically relate may gravitate toward you.

You can say what you mean but can you do what you say.

Action over words! Don't just speak about it, be about it!

SELF-LOVE

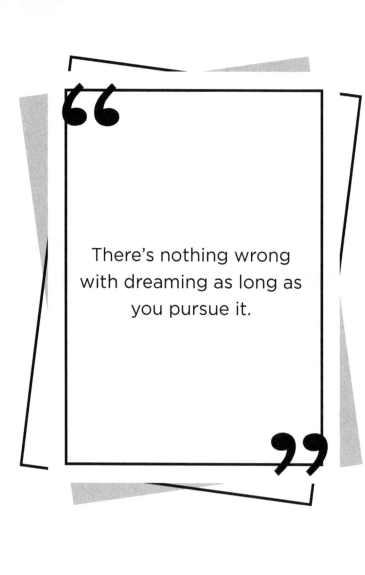

There's nothing wrong
with dreaming as long as
you pursue it.

What is the joy of dreaming if you don't go for it? They look good when you can imagine them, but they feel amazing when carrying them out. Dreams are often mis-understood and considered just imaginary thoughts. That's partially true. They are fantastic ideas with a desired destination which may take a little creativity to get there. Most of the time, there's nothing to lose but the inner voice that tells you that "you can't." The reality is that you can go for it, and many have succeeded.

Never be intimidated by the experience of others.

It doesn't matter how long they've been in the game. It matters how well you play the game when you enter.

You are self-affirmed when that callback didn't go any further but your drive to press even harder just turned up a notch!

When you are self-affirmed, nothing threatens your sense of confidence. You can walk in and out of any audition knowing you did the job that you were supposed to and everything else outside of your talent will work out. At the end of the day, you've already been affirmed and ready for whatever else comes your way. That's the mental mindset to strive for if you want to give your best shot every time.

STRATEGY/ PREPARATION

In the end, authenticity is key! Just keep it reel.

You can plan for anything as much as you'd like but there will always be uncharted territory or challenges that one may not anticipate. In the end, honesty is the best policy. Part of the audition experience can include questions from the casting directors. The purpose of these questions is often to help the casting director understand your choices better or maybe informative notes for them to use in their decision-making process. It's not a graded test, there are no right or wrong answers. Regardless of the purpose, which one may never be able to determine, always keep it authentic. By doing this, one never has to worry about giving the wrong answers because it is your truth. You can walk in and out of the room feeling less anxious because you know that going in, you will give the factual truth about yourself, and when you leave the room, you know for sure that you shared the facts as they applied to you. In the end, you gave it your all including your truth. If they can't accept that, then guess what; they are not ready to accept you. You don't ever want to feel like you earned an opportunity based on untruths because you will always find yourself anxious trying to keep up with a fib. This affects your happiness.

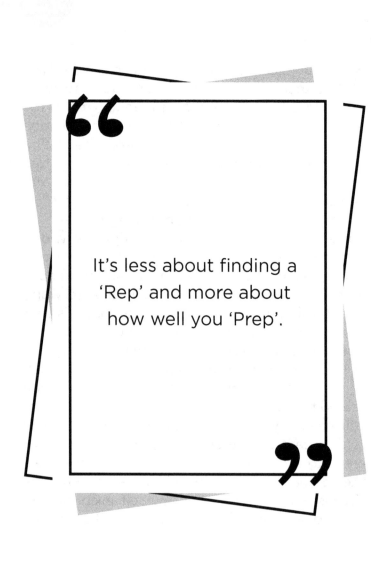

It's less about finding a 'Rep' and more about how well you 'Prep'.

Often enough, much effort goes into finding a representative (agent/manager), but not enough emphasis is spent on preparing one's profile. Many of the inquiries for representation are coming from aspiring Talent that believes his/her career starts with getting a rep. The reality is that your journey should begin well before you seek help from a rep. Actors should spend so much time prepping themselves that representatives notice them and are trying to recruit them to be on their roster.

Hard work beats talent when talent is hardly working.

It's great that you have talent. But talent alone is not going to win all the time. You have to wonder about those who have talent and work hard. If you want it more, you will have to work hard. If you don't mind losing it, you won't work as hard. Talent alone is not enough to sustain a prosperous journey of continued success in the acting arena.

Find your niche, and then dig deep.

We are all the same but very different. While striving for some of the same goals, discover your individuality or what is unique about you. Once you find it, find a way to use it for your advantage. After all, no one else can do it or have it quite like you. Instead of assimilating to become like the rest, find the strength in being different. Then and only then you will unleash the power of your uniqueness.

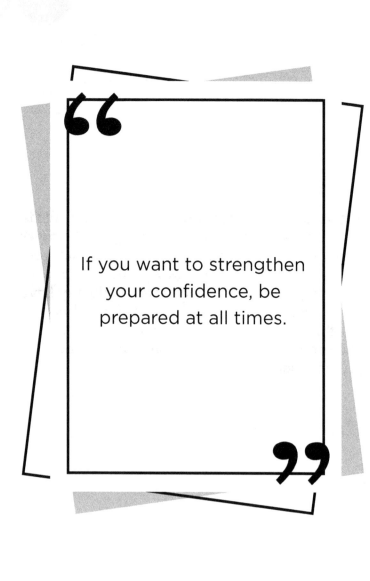

If you want to strengthen your confidence, be prepared at all times.

Keep your package updated. Be familiar with the latest trends. Grasp a complete understanding of the self tape setup. Know your lines. Be mentally prepared to receive and apply notes for adjustments. Read the trades regarding the latest news in the business.

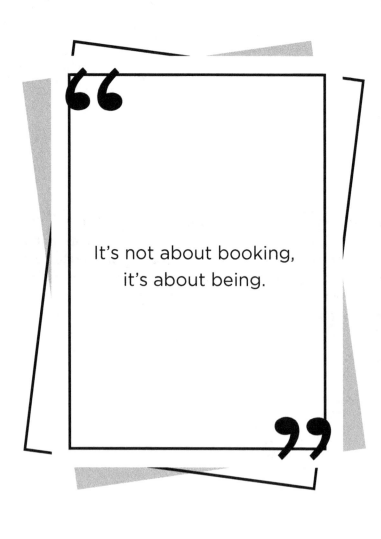

It's not about booking,
it's about being.

Establish your space on the market and booking is bound to come.

Practice makes
preparedness!

Practice leads to preparedness. Preparedness leads to confidence. Confidence manifests a powerful performance!

There you have it! Keep this resource close. Moreover, make sure you have it with you at every audition or
important meeting related to following your dreams.

ABOUT THE AUTHOR

Ronald "Wink" Woodall is the Founder and Chief Executive Officer of The Talent Connect (TTC) an entertainment service hub that offers Talent Management. He was once a childhood actor who currently has over 12 years of talent representation experience, as well as over 20 years of mental health counseling experience. TTC, under the leadership of Wink, serves as a motivational resource for the greater acting community. In addition to talent management, TTC offers motivational merchandise through its online store, career/mindset consultation for Talent, and motivational empowerment throughout all its platforms.

Wink's journey began in the 1980's when he joined the Black Spectrum Theater Company in Queens, NY as a childhood actor. It was during that time, under the guidance and leadership of Director Carl Clay, that he learned about his passion for the arts. In the theater program, he managed to audition and book several lead character roles in many productions for his age group; defining his craft to stand out amongst the rest. His performances garnered recognition from local newspapers and ultimately led him to book his first commercial, sponsored by the March of Dimes.

In the 1990s, as an aspiring talent, Wink joined Mollo Management Agency, which was known for launching the careers of stars like Lindsay Lohan,

Michelle Trachtenberg, & Tyler James Williams. He also participated in local print modeling campaigns and urban modeling events like BET's Rip the Runway. While he applied himself in the talent pool for acting and modeling, he also studied Education and Psychology at Hofstra University, where he took acting and entertainment business courses. As a student leader, Wink was appointed as a University Special Affairs Chairman for the African Peoples Organization (APO). This role and several other similar roles he acquired while in college not only introduced him to know how to secure talent for university events, but it initiated his journey of transitioning from pursuing performance-related goals to engaging his interest in talent representation. Wink graduated with a Bachelor of Arts in Psychology and eventually a Master of Science in Education (School Counseling).

With the overall experience of talent/business relations combined with a keen understanding of the social-emotional needs of "the working actor", Wink has carved out a niche for his unique style of representation. Some may refer to him as the "Industry Guidance Counselor." As business relations are a key element in navigating through the industry, Wink also incorporates his counseling background as a supportive feature while working with his clients. In the early 2000s, Wink initiated his Talent Management endeavors as he partnered with Actor Tobias Truvillion who eventually was nominated for an NAACP Image Award. Tobias was also the recipient of the prestigious AUDELCO award, a theater award bestowed among some of the finest African American legends like Denzel Washington, Wesley Snipes, Ozzie Davis, Ruby Dee, and several other icons.

In 2015, Wink launched TTC. It is currently a registered member of the national Talent Management Associa-tion. TTC is also a member of the talent representative Breakdown Services Ltd., which receives exclusive access to regional film, television, print, commercial, and theater casting listings nationwide. TTC's mission is to "connect" with others to define their talent and help them take the necessary steps to work up to their fullest potential. Self-love and motivation are among the core elements of TTC's motto. For Wink, connecting involves several components. Not only does Wink communicate frequently with talent agents, casting agents, and production creatives across the nation, but he also prides himself on forming strategic partnerships to help support the client's overall brand.

Overall, Wink is humbly thrilled to be involved in structuring the career paths of several working creatives both past and present, and looks forward to motivating and helping dedicated Talent connect the dots that will lead them toward finding their niche.

CPSIA information can be obtained
at www.ICGtesting.com
Printed in the USA
BVHW031149220922
647758BV00012B/1317